Francis

52 Multi-Let Tips

Valuable things come in small packages and this little book certainly proves that rule. The brilliant ideas contained herein are guaranteed to *Save You Stress, Time, Energy and Money* (S.Y.S.T.E.M.) and as an added bonus, your tenants *will love you!*

www.52MultiLetTips.com

The Smart Investors Guide

Artwork by Mary Andruseva
pinaple.artist@gmail.com

What do you want in life?

It's a question we all consider from time to time and the answer usually boils down to one thing, just to be happy!

That is what this book is, a little slice of happiness ☺

Have you ever walked into a house where the wallpaper is peeling away from the bare walls, a tap is dripping in the distance and the air is full of unknown odours! Yuck! Unloved houses are everywhere and they fill everyone with sadness, including the owners and especially the people who have to live there. It creates a spiralling circle of despondency!

But the truth is it doesn't really take much to turn a property into a warm, cosy and welcoming home that everyone can be proud of. It just takes a little more sustained effort to create a feeling of abundance that will really pay off for *everyone* in the long term.

To help you do that, we have painstakingly collected and put together 52 of the best property tips we could find from all corners of the UK. Why 52? Well there are 52 weeks in the year so we figured you could implement just one tip a week before moving on to the next, that way there is plenty of time and no need to feel overwhelmed.

We have integrated each and every one of these brilliant tips into our Multi-Let Cashflow System and they have without doubt made our lives somewhat easier and made the business more profitable.

Some of them you will already know and some you may choose to ignore, but we guarantee that these tips will help you create a better living environment for your customers, make you more money, make you at least 3 x's more efficient and 3 x's more successful a landlord than you are today, and hey, they maybe even make you a better person!

One thing for sure is that they will make *someone* happy!

So dive on in and tick off every Top Tip as you implement them. Oh and if you have any brilliant tips of your own that you would like to share, email us at

francis@multiletcashflowsystem.com

52 Multi-Let Tips

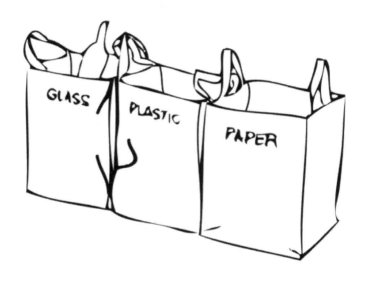

#1 Multi-Colour Plastic Recycling Bags

There is nothing worse than bottles, cans, bags and boxes overflowing all over the place! That's why every Multi-Let landlord who discovers these funky and brightly coloured bags just loves them!

You can't tell from the image but they are a very vibrant red, green and yellow.

Tenants also love them and they are guaranteed to help keep your Multi-Let neat and tidy. We would even go so far as to say that they are absolutely essential kit for every multi-let. They clip together and are available from Amazon at only £6!

Just type in 'Recycle Bags'.

Note - Tell your tenants not to put them outside with the bins – they are very desirable and you may find you are constantly replacing them!

#2 Your Most Important Team Member

This is a bigger Tip than most, but this is a VERY important subject. To say that your cleaner is one of the most essential members of your team is an absolute understatement, so taking your time to find the correct person is really essential. We once went through 7 cleaners in the space of 12 months (don't ask!) and this was a complete nightmare.

Each time there was a dispute, and each time it was a real problem getting all the keys returned. A few times we also felt the need to change the locks = bucket loads of unwanted hassle. We tried agencies, the small ads, English workers, foreign nationals, husband/wife teams, young mums, semi-retired, the lot!

So where is the best place to find a cleaner? Through bitter experience we would say 'word of mouth' and recommendations. Ask people you trust who they know, and always employ for an initial trial period. We have a simple two page agreement that we ask cleaners to sign. We also have a cleaners signing-in sheet at the property so we know they have been. No signature means no payment.

We often only visit our Multi-Lets once a month, so we ask our cleaner to report back anything she notices whilst in the house every fortnight. She is our 'spy on the ground'. This is a great way to monitor the property without constantly invading the privacy of your tenants. To ensure that everything is kept ship-shape we also ask the cleaner to pick up any rubbish at the front of the property and pop it in the bin.

Cleaners must also be prepared to monitor and clean mould (some won't due to using bleach) and to do the occasional extra hour here and there to retain standards. Ask your cleaner to clean the bathroom fans – they tend to collect dust and become inefficient. This will ensure better suction and less noise.

If you are ever strapped for time, you might want to consider asking your cleaner to take a photo of your gas and electric meter to send over to you, for the end-of-the-month readings. Not only will this save you time it will also confirm to you that the cleaner is at the house.

Our cleaner is even cool with letting tenants back into the house if ever they have forgotten their keys.

When you find a good cleaner do whatever it takes to hold onto them. We buy ours a nice hamper at Christmas and don't mind moving her cleaning days now and again if she has to be somewhere else.

In conclusion; Having a good cleaner is cool, but having a great one is absolutely ESSENTIAL!

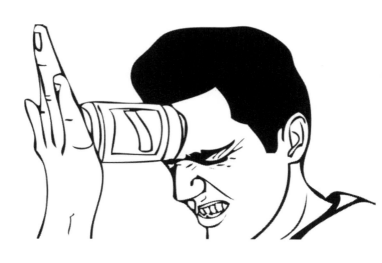

#3 Can Crushers

Ever seen a guy trying to impress a girl with a feat of strength? Like open a bottle of beer with their bare-teeth! Aggh! Try explaining that one to the dentist!

The chaps in your Multi-Let will just love the can-crusher! They will especially like crushing the cans when the ladies are around!

You can get them from Amazon often for £5 (can-crushers, not ladies!)

3 Smart Tips and don't ask us how we know this!

ok . . .

1. There are two sizes and you must get the bigger size for the taller cans

2. Make sure it is *REALLY* securely fixed to the wall! (Don't forget there is alcohol and possibly showing-off involved here – a dangerous mix!)

3. Put a plastic watertight bin underneath it to catch any drips and spillages, for when those macho guys are being over-zealous and trying to impress!

#4 I Can't Hold it Any Longer!

It will be a major benefit to install extra WC facilities in any property that has the space. You can usually squeeze them into areas that would otherwise be unused - the most common being under the stairs. In order to get the pipe-work to work in these restrictive spaces, we have used a system called Sani-flo. Using this system means that instead of the usual 100mm waste pipes, you can go as small as 22mm – and these pipes can even run vertically up the walls and out! Basically, more loo's = faster lets!

With larger models you can also run a shower off them.

An extra loo can often makes the difference when a prospective tenant is on the fence, and definitely worth the initial investment. We find the properties with more facilities rent faster and tenants stay longer = a better business model. We usually supply all materials and a good plumber can do the installation in a day at a cost of around £200.

If you are *really* tight for space you can fit an all-in-one WC and basin (yep the basin is in the lid of the WC) available from B&Q for £120.

You may also need to fit an extractor fan to comply with building regs.

#5 Skype Viewings

If your tenant market includes some foreign nationals moving to the UK, or people unable to view in person, then this is HUGE and will play a major part in eradicating *ALL* voids for you. This Top Tip has saved us *sooo* much time, energy and money.

As you would expect, you arrange a Skype viewing with the potential tenant so that they can view the house 'live' and say *hi* to a few of your nice existing tenants.

You will find that many Skyp'ers take the rooms on the spot.

Why does it work?

Because they can see the current condition of the property, not some 5 year old photo. (As if you would do that!) They get to interact with you (and see how wonderful you are!) and also get to chat with your lovely tenants. (Arrange for the best ones to be home!) Job done!

But like many things in life the devil is in the detail, and we have dedicated a section of our popular mini-manual 'Endless Tenants' to exactly this. Whereas most people stick up an ad on Spareroom and hope for the best, we are much more proactive and have identified 17 ways to fill a room.

Endless Tenant contains every tactic, every strategy and every trick that we use to ensure we have consistently full rooms - in fact we have not had a void, even for an hour, for longer than we can remember.

It contains sections on;

- ✓ Filling your rooms fast
- ✓ Creating a buzz
- ✓ Social Media
- ✓ Which website
- ✓ Old school marketing
- ✓ Websites
- ✓ Building a list
- ✓ Keeping your ad at the top
- ✓ How to use videos
- ✓ 9 must-do's before a viewing
- ✓ 15 questions to get the perfect tenant
- ✓ The best way to say 'no thanks'
- ✓ Group viewings – yes or no
- ✓ Our referencing method
- ✓ Who is Pepper the purple puppy?
- ✓ Meet the housemates . . . or not
- ✓ The 3ft rule
- ✓ The 'no-voids' mindset

Get it from the website:

www.MultiLetCashflowSystem.com

#6 Water Pressure

This very important tip for Multi-Let living. Whenever you are looking at a potential property, a quick and basic test to ensure the water pressure won't be problematic is to turn the shower on and flush the toilet at the same time. Does the flow rate reduce significantly? Ok this is just a quick test.

You could also take a 1 litre container with you to test the water pressure. Turn a ground floor cold water tap full on. If it takes more than 7 seconds to fill, there may be a problem. This is a fast and rough test.

It's better to spot this now than when all the tenants have moved in and start complaining about cold showers!!

There are several ways to fix this including the highly expensive option of getting larger bore pipe installed to feed the property.

If you think it may be a problem, consult with your plumber and get an overdraft facility set up!

#7 Standing Orders from Day One

We have a company policy of 'minimum input for maximum output'.

When new tenants move in, we insist they set up their Standing Order's (SO) for the rent to **arrive** in our bank account on the first day of the month. This way we only have to check the bank once each month – on the 2nd day of the month.

If the move-in date is less than 50% of the way through the month we just ask the tenant to pay pro-rota for the remainder of the month. If it is over 50% of the way through the month, we ask for the following month's rent, plus the remainder of the current month. This way we ensure we just have to check the bank once a month to make sure everyone's paid. Cool.

Some tenants will try and persuade you to set the SO on 'their' pay-day. Tell them sorry, but its company policy. (Computer says no!) We did consider using a Direct Debit system, but this is not free and all those little fees can add up to a whopper! But if you want to give it a go try www.landlordsrent.co.uk

We have a consistent 100% success rate with this simple system.

Cash payments: Taking cash payments has drawbacks.

1. The tenant not being there at the agreed time to meet you, which is totally frustrating.

2. They might say they have left it somewhere for you to collect and it goes 'missing' = big problems.

3. . . . it's just more unnecessary work!!

We seem to be moving closer to a cash-less society every day, with more and more options for taking payments on hand-held card machines becoming available. We know some people who are using an App called Smart Trade and say it is a really simple and really good system. You punch in some details and then scan the tenants card. They type the cards security code into your phone and the payment is made.

This may be great for taking holding fees when a tenant wants to secure a room on the spot. It will also be good if you take cash payments. We don't.

Check it out here: www.smarttradeapp.com.

Conclusion: Standing Orders are simple, free, everyone understands them and they work, so why complicate it?

#8 How to Find an Endless Supply of Quality Tenants

Someone once said 'Property investing would be a brilliant industry to work in if it weren't for . . . tenants!'

Tenants are like Bovril – you either love 'em or hate 'em. But however you feel about them, you need them to fill your rooms, pay the rent and hopefully fund the lifestyle you want to live!

To say that we here at MLCS HQ hate voids would be an understatement. We totally detest them, and a while ago we decided to do something about it! We brainstormed, researched, interviewed investors and agents, we tried and we tested, we did some crazy stuff and in the end created a multitude of systems to ensure our voids were reduced to an absolute minimum, and then to zero.

Fast forward and we literally cannot remember the last time we had a void! This is an incredible industry record and one we are keen to maintain at all costs and so will do whatever it takes. We have even filled a room on the impossible date of December 24th using the cool systems we have created! By mid-day there was no room at the Inn!

We decided we just couldn't keep this insider knowledge to ourselves and so have bottled it all up and created the brilliant Endless Tenants [as per #5] mini-manual. Lots of landlords are already utilising the information it contains up and down the UK to help them eliminate voids forever. .

Extra Tip: If you are not 100% sure about the person who turns up for a viewing, always say *'You are not the first; we're waiting to hear back from some other guys'*. This way if you decide not to take them, there are no awkward conversations as to why you refused them.

The first thing you must do is adopt a 'NO VOIDS' mindset. If we have an empty room coming up we are on it like a dog with a bone. This is where the money is and this is what buys you the nice clothes and well earned holidays. Too many people accept 5% or even 10% voids. Multiply this by your growing number or rooms and the many years you will be working in the industry and you are talking a LOT of money!

You must learn to attack voids with a vengeance!

The crazy stuff? That would be our 'French Dancers and Trainee Firemen' strategy for filling new houses! This is something we have done a few times and it works every time without fail, if it is a new house with the first few viewings.

How to shop ebaY like a NINJA!

#9 Furnishing a House for Next to Nothing

This Top Tip is a great big tease!

What would you think if I told you we spend a tiny fraction of what most landlords spend on furnishing a property, and we do it by making just one phone call? We never see or touch the furniture until we visit the new property to inspect it.

Most people don't believe me and dismiss it as some cheap marketing ploy – we do run a training company after all. Hey-ho!

Our best purchases to date has been two *'as good as new'* leather, 3 seater sofas for £11.50 each, and a 42" flat-screen TV for £26 - that's way less than a £1 an inch!! These savings are not unusual with the system we use!

We use eBay but we never actually buy anything on the website itself - we use a second website to do that. We don't even collect the purchases, this is also totally systemised via a third website.

Are we going to tell you how . . . sadly not! It fills 4 pages of our legendary training manual – too much for these small Top Tips booklet. A lady on one event said this information alone was worth the cost of the course! We agree! We never buy new these days and always use our 'system'!

Well that's the end of the 'teaser' – all available within the now legendary MLCS full event Manual.

Here are some other top eBay tips:

Snag an eBay Bargain

Auctions that end during normal working hours - 8am till 6pm have less people bidding on them as do auctions that end at 2 or 3 o'clock in the morning, so can be cheaper. Whereas evenings, weekends and holidays have many more bidders and this often pushes the prices up.

To locate auctions that finish in the dead of night, use 'Crazy End Time' search.

Other good sub categories to check out include 'Local Bargains', 'Unwanted Gift' and 'Ending Now'.

Misspelt adverts

People with fat fingers may list an item as a 'qardrobe' or a 'xouble bed'. No one will be looking at these listings and you may be the only bidder. Try these links - www.fatfingers.co.uk, www.goofbay.com

Last minute auctions

If you are collecting, check the area. If not, get delivery charges, as you may spend all you have saved on getting the item delivered! www.lastminute-auction.com

Local to You

Pick-up only deals have fewer bids and so are cheaper but you can't normally search for collection items only – until now! We discovered a free new tool that locates them. Here is the (long) link – http://www.moneysavingexpert.com/shopping/local-ebay-deals/

Search and destroy!

If you can't find what you are looking for, set a 'favourite search' and eBay will email each time a seller lists the item you're after.

Simply type a product in eBay's own search bar, such as "solid pine chest of drawers" or "42" plasma TV", and click 'save search'. Be as specific as possible for the most accurate results. Then, when someone lists the item, an email will pop into your inbox.

These top tips are totally guaranteed to save you £1,000's over the years as they have for us!

#10 Pulling Weeds!

From our first ten Rent 2 Rent properties we initially made just short of £5,000 net per month. Twelve months later we were making over £6,000 from these same ten properties.

How did we do that? We continued with upgrades in all properties and at the end of the year we had either raised the rent for all new tenants or issued a Section 13 to existing tenants to enable us to increase their rent.

With all Assured Shorthold Tenancies that have become periodic tenancies [the tenant has been with you for longer than six months] you can automatically increase the rent after twelve months if it is agreed and signed in the tenancy agreement, or if the tenant laterally agrees to the increase.

However, if the increase is not stated in the agreement and the tenants dispute the increase, The Housing Act 1988 still enables landlords to increase the rent after the initial fixed term, by issuing a section 13 notice to the tenant.

Of course we want to be fair to our tenants but let's not forget that we are in business to make money, and this means regular rent reviews. Tweaking our rents meant an annual increase of £12k on just these 10 properties. What would you do with your £12k?

Equally, if the tenant thinks you are trying to charge an excessive rent, he has every right to complain to the local council, who will send in their SWAT team to assess a fair level of rent. This could go either way . . . but don't hold your breath.

We were talking with a local investor who was surprised at out rent levels and said he had not increased his for years. It seemed to us he was throwing away bucket loads of money. If he was collecting more rent, he could reinvest some of that money into the property and charge higher rents for a higher spec house. It's a virtuous circle.

We are forever looking for ways to tweak everything for constant and never ending improvement.

Think of your business as a beautiful garden and you are the gardener. You have a beautiful looking garden because you are forever pulling a weed here and a weed there. You are constantly adjusting and recalibrating for maximum efficiency and you make it all look so effortless and easy from the outside.

#11 Is your property really safe?

Is your property safe? Would you let the person you love more than anything in the whole world, spend a night there?

OK let's not kid ourselves – the worst case scenario is that you have a fire and someone dies or gets seriously injured!

You *MUST,* without fail, make the safety of your tenants your number one priority and make sure annual gas safety checks, 5 year electric safety checks and periodic fire alarm tests (this may vary depending on your local council) and Portable Appliance Test (PAT) certificates are bang up to date. You should build simple reminders into your systems - it's easy to do it and easy not to do it – it's your choice!

This doesn't mean they can be neglected in between dates! Have a simple safety tick-list as part of your interim inspection sheet. You can also ask the tenants and your cleaner to report any faults/damages immediately.

We ask our selected tradesmen to inform us of our annual checks as a double-whammy fail safe. This also means they will probably get the job.

We have heard that some people hard wire appliances so that a PAT is not required. We did consider hard wiring irons after a few went missing, but eventually decided against it!

Providing your customers with a living environment that they can feel safe in must be your number one priority. This is *THE* most important aspect of running a property business, so you must give it your undivided attention . . . or you may just find yourself living in one of those Government run Multi-Lets :-(

#12 Non Paying Tenants

You rent rooms to make money to create a better life or to buy you nice stuff, right? When tenants don't pay, you don't get your nice stuff, and that sucks!

So, you must have a clear plan of action, and act on it immediately EVERY time a payment is late. We have a precise and definite process, and if occasionally a payment is missed, we don't have to stop and think as we know exactly what we have to do, and so consequently we very rarely have a late payment.

Our policy is -

Day one - A text and a reminder that SO's are obligatory

Day two - Telephone. If no response, email and text

Day four - Visit tenant. If tenant is not home, text and pin 1st late payment letter to their bedroom door.

Day six - Post 2nd late payment letter and call/text and possibly call guarantor.

You should always listen politely to your tenant's reason (the best one we heard was 'my cat caught fire!') as to why their rent is late, and possibly make allowances (your call). Then you must firmly state your company policy of *'No-Pay, No-Stay'* - and strictly adhere to it, after all you still have to pay YOUR mortgage/lease.

In fact, by being lenient, you could be just training your tenants to be late with any future rental payments!

p.s. It is not legally acceptable for tenants to withhold any payments due to repairs pending. Equally, landlords cannot issue a Section 21 to evict a tenant who is complaining about essential repairs, until those repairs are complete.

We have a whole section on this in our MLCS manual and have not had a non-payer for longer than we can remember = our systems work!!

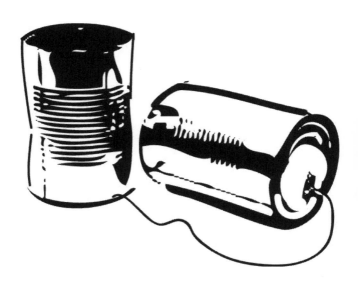

#13 Does it Matter What They Think of You?

Are you a good Landlord/Agent?

Keeping the information flowing goes a long way to keeping your customers (tenants) happy. You must never forget that although it's your house, it's their home!

Let them know your long-term planned upgrades and especially let them know when you are carrying out bigger maintenance jobs. Showing them that you care and respect them, will leave no room for any misunderstandings and will also go a long way to keeping your customers happy, which will in turn increase your bottom line. Don't wait for them to complain – do any repairs before they even notice them. You might even want to pop in at Christmas with a box of Quality Street, some beers or a set of fairy lights! (Don't forget the PAT!)

Why is any of this important?

Research says most room sharers stay put for an average of 9 months (This is increasing). This means every 9 months you have to get busy getting a new tenant. We REALLY look after our customers and they stay for an average 18 months = less work, more time to grow the business and more profits and free time for us in the long term!

If you don't mind the extra work, then changing tenants every 9 months might work well for you, after all you get more admin fees. But less tenant change overs means that we can spend more time actually building our business and setting up more properties, and this ultimately will make us a lot more money than we could make from admin fees.

So the bottom line is, be prepared to go the extra mile, look after your customers and they will look after you (mostly).

#14 Zero Tolerance

We operate a 100% Zero-tolerance policy when it comes to smoking in the house. This may seem harsh but we do it for two reasons.

1. It's against the law and 2. It's the major cause of deaths in house fires!

The rules are plain and anyone who chooses to flaunt them is shown the door – no second chance. You may find that some guys smoke 'funny-cigarettes' – we have also heard this called 'wacky-backy', and for obvious reasons they don't want to smoke outside, so they will hang out of the windows! You will have to be extra vigilant!

Our really cool house rules, the tenants *'Guide to Living'* (available from the MLCS website as a free download on the manuals page) also states that any smokers must not sit in an open window or stand in the doorway and let smoke drift into the house – they must step outside and close the door (umbrellas provided). Why should anyone have to breathe another person's smoke! Make no exceptions, take no prisoners and show no mercy!!!

Note; You MUST include a 'No smoking in ANY part of the house' clause in your AST to make it enforceable.

#15 Rotate Your Pictures

. . . and we don't mean turn them up-side down – that would be silly!

Here is a simple and quick tip that is often overlooked and can leave your tenants feeling somewhat unloved if you choose to ignore it.

Periodically we will swap the large canvas prints in the communal areas between houses. This keeps everyone interested, it shows the tenant's that we care and is good for the soul!

We find that tenants love those big bold bad-boy Banksy prints, available from eBay.

Is it worth the effort?

As per Tip #14, tenants stay in our properties twice as long as the average tenancy and we also get lots of recommendations. We are playing the long game here, so yes, all the little touches ARE worth the extra effort :-)

#16 AST's or Licences?

This old chestnut keeps rolling around so we'll keep it short.

The general consensus of the benefit of using licenses instead of AST's, is that you can evict on a very short notice period, in fact we have even heard of 'instant dismissal'. (*Pack your bags and go*, type of thing!)

For a licence to be used, additional criteria must be met, such as providing other specific services to the tenant. In essence a license is only 'permission to occupy', as used in a B&B and if that permission is withdrawn, so then are the person's legal rights. But unless this specific criteria is met, in the eyes of the law a license is fundamentally the same as an AST. A judge once famously said – *'you can call it a mobile earth-relocation device', but in the eyes of the law it's still a spade!* (Or something along those lines!)

For an AST to be used the property must be the principal residence, so you may think a license is therefore OK if the tenant goes home on weekends?

If you DO use a license and illegally evict someone, this can come back to bite you at ANY time in the future, and with a 'no-win no-fee' culture becoming more prevalent in the UK, it's really not worth the risk.

We only use AST's. We are always extremely choosey who we let into our properties (and our lives!) and to date have never had to evict a Multi-Let tenant. We have assisted the odd bad apple tenant to move on, by finding them similar rooms nearby, offering to pay for a removal van and even offering a part month rent free or a few bottles of wine. This is usually the fastest and most efficient way to resolve situations where a tenant is simply a bad fit.

Incidentally, any clause you add to your contracts must be reasonable and fair to be enforceable. 'No strangers in your room and lights out by 9.30' may not stand up in court!

Ps – There are 17 grounds for eviction and if you get it wrong it can get a bit like Snakes and Ladders. *Do not pass Go and do not collect £200*! (Whoops, wrong game!) We have an eviction specialist in our MLCS support group with a 100% unblemished record and always take his advice. Our advice: If you are unsure, consult the experts.

Our conclusion; as there is no legal requirement to have an actual written contract with a tenant, it doesn't really matter what you call it. Using a licence to remove a tenants legal rights is unacceptable but apart from that, it really doesn't matter because the law will protect them and a well worded AST with fair conditions and enforceable terms will protect the landlord.

#17 Tenants Just LOVE Big Maps

You can only hang *so* many big canvas prints in a house. We bought some giant maps and the tenants really love them. Lots of our guys are graduates and they love to chat about their gap year travels. They are also a great conversational piece when you are doing viewings. We tear the edges of ours and stick them to the walls with wallpaper paste.

If this is your first time it might be a good idea to get assistance mixing the paste and sticking it on the wall.

Or you could go one better and install a giant wall mural. Just go to Amazon.co.uk and type in what you are looking for – there are lots out there and they will certainly give a room the wow factor!

For this one we definitely recommend getting it done by a professional.

#18 Is It OK to Snoop?

AKA Interim Inspections! It's so easy to overlook this area – we are all busy people after all. Doing regular inspections 3 to 4 months apart are essential to problem-free and well run households. The tenants know you are never far away and will treat the property with respect. You will also catch any problems early, stop them from escalating and therefore not give tenants a reason to withhold the rent. (Outstanding maintenance issues is the number one reason for tenants mistakenly attempting to withhold rent)

You must diarise these at the start of each year and stick to them. If you have multiple properties, do them all on one/several consecutive days. Have your report sheet ready, and don't forget to inform all tenants that you are coming at least 24 hours in advance and that will need access to the whole house, including the bedrooms.

#19 Must-Have Key-Safes

If you own or control a Multi-Let property then you MUST fit one of these in the vicinity of the front door! We chose to pay a little extra and go for police approved safes as this had a favourable impact on the insurance payments. We also opted for the additional plastic cover that makes it look like a BT box and a small metal plate fitted to the interior to stop the number being changed by tradesmen etc (but this may just be us being paranoid!) Prices are from £50 on Amazon.

Who are they for? Tradesmen, tenants who have lost a key and possibly new tenants moving in late on a Sunday night - it's all about leveraging your time!

"I've lost my keys . . . again!"

These are the words that every landlord dreads as it usually involves wasting your valuable time, time that you will never get back!

One gentleman in our support group was having a major problem with tenants losing keys. He had a key safe with the front door key so that the tenant can let themselves in which was great. He asked 'then what - how do they get into their room?'

He suggested a further key safe within the house with all keys, but this would be a big security risk and so is a no-go.

We advised him to get 5 cheap key safes and fix them onto a plank of wood, which he would securely fix to a wall under the stairs. Each safe has a key for one bedroom. When a tenant calls to say they are locked out, he gives them the code for the external safe and the relevant room safe. Cool!

We reminded him to change the codes after every use.

We have only had one lost key in 3 years and he couldn't understand why he had so many problems until I told him we charge £25 for lost keys. It's not the cost of the key it's the time and hassle to replace them.

S.Y.S.T.E.M

Saves Your Stress, Time, Energy & Money

EMPLOYING
YOUR PROPERTY
MANAGER

... For Free

#20 Employing Your Property Manager... For Free!

How did this one manage to be at # 20? This is probably one of the most important parts of the Multi-Let puzzle! Here at MLCS HQ we often say that there is a big difference between building a *'Business'* and creating a *'Busy-Mess'*! It's so easy to get caught up doing all the things that could and should be out-sourced, just to *'make sure it's done properly'*! Agghh! We did this for way too long!

If you haven't already read The E-Myth by Michael Gerber, you need to do that immediately. It's a classic book that details how you should be working 'on' your business and not 'in' your business. Next — even before you secure your first Multi-Let property — read our Employing Your Property Manager . . . *for free,* mini-manual. You may be surprised to learn that you can afford a manager from the first day of setting up your Rent 2 Rent business, *IF* you structure their employment as we have.

Going down the traditional route of allowing your rooms to be managed by an external agent means you lose any admin fee and pay the agent a % on top. The way we do it, our property manager actually brings money *IN* to the business and grows with us as part of our team.

Inside you will find;

- ✓ Your property managers profile
- ✓ The hiring process
- ✓ Where to advertise
- ✓ The advert
- ✓ Where to hold the interview
- ✓ The interview
- ✓ The contract
- ✓ The handover period
- ✓ Access to the bank
- ✓ Safeguard against poaching
- ✓ How is it free?

To make it really easy for you we include a link to a secret page on the Multi Let Cashflow System website where you can download

- ✓ Property manager manual template
- ✓ Self employed contract
- ✓ Disguised employee
- ✓ HMRC employers guidelines

This important Mini-Manual and other material are available on the MLCS website to help you on your property journey. They will definitely allow you to spend more time sat on the beach or doing whatever it is that you like doing best!

#21 LED Lighting

It's a painful experience walking into a shop to buy a load of LED light bulbs to replace some other perfectly good light bulbs! BUT when you see your electric bill a month or so later, and a big cheesy grin spreads across your face, it will all be worth it.

In fact, it is estimated that LED lighting 'can' reduce your bills by up to 80%! Wow – why would anyone not install LED's? It's another of those *'Just do it'* moments! Watch out for cheap imports that easily break and have a limited life. Also watch out for Top Multi Let Tip # 50, which spells out how to not only get the remaining 20% free, but to also put some money into your bank!

If it's too painful to do the whole house in one go, just do the communal areas first. You might also consider motion detector light bulbs to save even more money. Yes they do exist and they will probably annoy the hell out of your less animated tenants!

We have seen timed light switches on stairs and other places where people are just passing through. But our thinking is that you would have a lot of explaining to do if someone had an accident on a darkened stairway.

Try www.ledhut.co.uk or your local B&Q or Wickes for any special offers.

#22 Solving Seasonal Damp Problems

Some older properties are often prone to damp issues at certain times of the year. If you can't afford the big expensive fix, you can try a number of cheaper ones:

1. HG Mould Spray. £5 from B&Q (buy one!)

2. Mould-proof paint www.glixtone.com £25-50

3. Mid range Dehumidifier £55 to £125 Amazon

4. Envirovent Fan £230 www.envirovent.com

When you are cleaning the area, always use a bleach based cleaner and make sure to open the window! Some people say that a wipe over with white wine vinegar will neutralise the mould and inhibit re-growth.

We have a whole section on Damp and Condensation in our tenants house rules – we call it the *'Guide to Living'* and it's available FREE from the MLCS website – click on the 'manuals' tab and download.

Top tip; whenever you visit the seaside or a forest, breathe deeply - there is nothing better than clean fresh air!

#23 Appoint a Sheriff

If you have a problem house – nothing serious, just lots of niggly whinges and complaints (like that old favourite who's turn is it to put the bins out?) it may be a good idea to deputise one of your tenants!

Some tenants are like naughty children and just need a bit of guidance and a leader to follow. They probably just miss their mummy and daddy!

We have done this a few times and we reduced the sheriffs rent by £20 a month in exchange for them being responsible for keeping on top of everything in the house, including bins, cleanliness, reporting tenant issues etc. If they are doing a great job we also slip the odd bottle of moonshine into their kitchen cupboard.

Rules; There are always rules! They mustn't tell the other housemates that they have been deputised or that they are getting perks as this causes dissension in the ranks. We also had to deal with this and had to ask the sheriff to hand his badge back and resign. This caused some disgruntlement and he decided to saddle up and ride off into the sunset!

So be careful who you deputise.

#24 Apply the 3ft Rule

A quick one at #24 and maybe a bit obvious to some!

Don't know what the 3ft Rule is?

If you are looking for a new Multi-Let, for tenants, for tradesmen etc, then you MUST apply the 3ft Rule!

We have been literally given deals that are making us £££'s by friends and friends of friends. If they didn't know what we were doing or what our business was, they wouldn't have been able to offer them to us!!

So tell EVERYONE in your community, everyone you know, friends, family, the postman, the cat, the dog, the local shopkeeper – EVERYONE - about what you do and what you are looking for.

The power of word of mouth is one of the strongest and cheapest advertising tools that you have, and is often overlooked by most. While you are at it, don't forget to post on that thing called 'Social Media'.

#25 The Rotating DVD Library

We used to think that the best way to get our customers (tenants) to like us was to charge them a really low admin fee. This was great for the soul but bad for business. These days we charge a bigger admin fee and our customers still like us (we think!)

A great way to show you *really care* is to create a small DVD library in each house. We donated our own unwanted DVD's, asked all our family and friends to make a donation, picked up a few Amazon bargains as well as any we spotted in second hand shops.

The tenants add their own, and from time to time we will rotate them between the houses and usually receive an email or two of gratitude. Get a small bookcase/shelve from eBay and don't allow tenants to overload it with trashy videos– stay in control!

It is said that 'poor' people fill their bookcases with DVD's, whilst the 'rich' fill theirs with books!

I wonder if they have a copy of Mayhem, Murder and Multi-Lets?

www.mayhemmurderandmultilets.com

#26 Change-Over Day

If you apply all you have learnt from the Endless Tenants mini-manual, and adopt a *'no voids'* mind-set, you will without a doubt, be consistently earning more from your properties than most other landlords.

To maximise you income you will also need to have a clear system for the change-over day to make this a slick *'no thinking needed'* process. This starts with telling departing tenants that they must be gone by 12 noon, and incoming tenants not to arrive before 5pm.

So you have a 5 hour window of opportunity.

This is our simple procedure:

Check room PRIOR to the move out day.
11.50 – Sign out tenant and inspect room.
12.00 – If necessary meet handyman at house with all materials and a tick list of any jobs.
1pm - 2pm – Cleaner arrives to make sure room is spotless while you double check all new paperwork.
2pm - 5pm – Sign new tenant in

You may be tempted to leave a day or so to give plenty of time to carry out any refurb etc, but this really is unnecessary and could cost you many £1K's over the years. Think *'Military Campaign'* and make sure and get all those ducks in a row! Make it fun if you like.

Of course it doesn't always go to plan, sometimes tenants are slow leaving or arrive early, and Murphy's Law dictates that this will be the room that needs the most attention. In these cases we help to move possessions into the living room, while we work at double speed sorting the bedroom. Don't let a tenant move into a less than perfect room, or it'll be much less than perfect when they move out!

What to do if a tenant says he has decided to stay a few more days and you already have the new tenants all lined up to move in?

Check out tip #47, you'll love it!

#27 Essential Pre-Viewing Prep

Arriving at the house at least 10 minutes early could actually save you hours in wasted repeat viewings. Prior to a viewing, we always tell the tenants to have a tidy up and we arrive early to ensure the house smells nice and is looking good. Some people are fussy about their surrounding and their housemates.

You know the old cliché – *You never get a second chance to make a first impression'!*

We find that dressed bedrooms are *always* the first to go and we have large carrier bags that hold the 'dressing kits'. Keep them basic – duvet cover, pillows, a few cushions, a small rug and perhaps a plastic flower in a vase. We may place a lamp here and there but never leave them as that incurs more cost when you need to get a PAT certificate for them.

Don't forget to straighten all the artwork!

We have identified the 9 essentials that you *MUST* do before any viewing and have detailed them in the Endless Tenants mini-manual available from the MLCS website.

When you arrive at the property, imagine you are seeing it for the very first time and ask yourself the question "would I live here?"

We like to feel proud of our properties and making these extra little efforts before each viewing can make the difference between a tenant taking the room or you having to trudge around another 4+ viewings, and we are sure you have much better things to do with your time!

Remember your new mantra

MINIMUM INPUT FOR MAXIMUM OUTPUT

PS Don't forget to collect your room dressing kits when the room has been let. In the early days we completely forgot about a few dressing kits and then all the other tenants started asking for artwork and soft furnishings!

#28 Negotiate *Everything*

When taking on a Rent 2 Rent deal, the only thing you can negotiate is the rent —right? We used to think this way but not anymore — all thanks to the many guys and girls that have come through our MLCS training! Some of them have even managed to get the owners to pay the monthly gas and electric bills! (crazy!) We have never been able to do that, but we have negotiated a free month's rent at the beginning of the tenancy, furniture upgrades, new carpets, decorating and no deposits amongst many other things.

These days we never assume anything — you never know what you can get unless you ask! Always start with a blank sheet and work out a deal that is fair for everyone. It's a good idea to have a couple of *'throw-a-ways'* held in reserve that you can *'give'* to the property owner in return for something that you really want. If you have completed the MLCS training, remember to use the totally awesome and powerful MLCS negotiation formula.

A great little book that digs deep into negotiation skills is Simon Hazeldine's *Bare Knuckle Negotiating* available from Amazon.co.uk

Simons says that if your first offer brings forth gasps of outrage from the other party, it's a good starting point! ;-)

#29 Is Your Head in The Clouds?

If you still think clouds are white fluffy things that float in the sky – think again!

These days you simply cannot ignore cloud technology. 'Cloud' refers to applications, services or resources made available to users on demand via the Internet, from a cloud computing provider's servers.

You can utilise cloud-based computing as a way to increase capacity, enhance functionality or add additional services on demand without having to commit to potentially expensive infrastructure costs or train existing in-house support staff.

We have our joint area of the cloud – accessible by any team member from any device, from anywhere in the world. We also have private areas and areas where we can grant access to selected people for a period of time.

Industry experts say that in a few years everything will be cloud based, so it's a good idea to get up to speed right now - the possibilities are vast. You will also be secure in the knowledge that should your computer ever seriously crash - all your precious files and photos can be safely retrieved.

A few years ago we had a serious crash with one of our computers. We had a friend who worked for the police and so asked if their special hard drive recovery department could retrieve it.

If they couldn't do it, no one could, and guess what … they couldn't do it, and I lost a year of work including lots of photos because I had failed to back it all up. Doh!

Now that we are cloud based this will never happen again, as it is saved in multiple and totally secure locations (as well as the separate hard-drive sat on my desk!).

There are many options available – Dropbox, Google Drive and Box to name a few. We have been using Egnyte for several years. The future is here so jump onboard and get used to it now. Just do it!

#30 Deposits 101

We use Deposit Protection Service (DPS) and do not hold the deposits ourselves. There two reasons for this.

The first one is that this service is free! Some guys prefer to keep the deposits in their own bank. You are not allowed to spend this money and you must pay for the privilege of keeping it, so why bother. Free is much better in our books!

The second reason is that it creates a 'barrier' between you and the tenant in the case of a dispute. Telling the tenant that their money is held in a Government backed scheme, and that they must follow the claim procedure, brings forth a much better reaction than informing them that YOU have THEIR money in YOUR bank! Trust us!

You must protect the deposit within 30 days and must issue the tenant with their 'Prescribed Information', 'Terms and Conditions' and 'A Tenants Guide'. A failure to do this could cost you big time!

DPS is a simple system to master. You can secure deposits on the spot using your mobile phone to access the website and also refund them on check-out day if the tenant is with you. Check out their website here;

www.depositprotection.com

#31 Small Utility Bills = More Holidays!

Do you find sorting the utilities a bore? Us too, but the more money we save, the more holidays we can take, so we spend a chuck of time minimising bills.

In the early days our Multi-Lets had multiple utility bills, which were a real headache and always took a lot of sorting out. As our portfolio of properties grew we knew we had to find a better solution than having multiple suppliers, each with their own way of doing things.

Then we discovered Utility Warehouse – a service provider that combines ALL of your utilities for each house together onto one simple monthly bill! There is also a cash-back card which enables you to reduce your personal monthly charges – sometimes substantially – whenever you buy food, fuel and a thousand other things. Many people overlook this when they are considering which provider to use for their properties. Using the cash-back card we often reduce our personal monthly utility bill to single figures.

They don't yet provide TV or water yet but . . . we hear it is in the pipeline! (Boom Boom!) For more information on how to save money, make money and get your expensive utilities under control, email jane@multiletcashflowsystem.com

New generation smart meters will be fitted in most households by 2020. With a smart meter you can see how much energy you're using and what you're spending in pounds and pence. You'll get accurate bills from your energy supplier – no more estimated bills. This has to be a good thing!

Ps. Look out for Multi-Let Tip # 50, it will tell you how to get a FREE electric supply (we have just done this) and the good news is that there are another 19 cool MLCS Tips in between!

#32 Start a Team-Document

We once read that the only consistent thing in life, is change. This may be somewhat of an oxymoron, but never a truer word was spoken. Everything changes over time and just when you have a great maintenance team all lined up, they are either too busy somewhere else, gone back to Uni, on a long holiday, taking care of their sick mum, broke their leg ski-ing or changed their phone number and forget to tell anyone! (We've had them all!)

These days we have a Maintenance Team-Document in our cloud that anyone can add to and edit. We are always asking for recommendations (this is the best way to find good trades people) and will sometimes take a photo of a good looking vehicle (check out the van interior - a tidy van usually indicates an organised person) and record the details when we get back to the office.

We always have at least 3 each of; plumbers, gas engineers, tilers, electricians, PAT guys, fast painters, carpenters, cleaners and deep cleaners (more expensive), rubbish clearance guys, bin power-washers, window repair guy, window cleaners, carpet and sofa cleaners, second hand appliances suppliers, gardeners, locksmiths, printers, leafleters and of course a really good and reliable general handy person.

If your handyperson is a good all rounder, they will be worth their weight in gold and you must do whatever is necessary to hold onto them!

A great way to do this is to be a fast payer. As soon as the job is done, have a quick check to see that it is up to your standard, its complete and the area has been left neat and tidy (train your tradesmen to do this and it will save you lots of time over the years!)

Starting a Team Document does not always seem so important when you are starting out or if everything is trucking along nicely, but when you need them you usually need then RIGHT NOW, and this is when you will slip into panic mode . . . unless you have an updated 'Team-Document' that you can begin to call.

#33 The *YouTube* Explosion

Videos are fast becoming the favoured way to advertise rooms. Owned by Google and with 1 Billion users per month, You Tube's revenue was $5.6 billion in 2014, up 51% from $3.7 billion in 2013, and that's significantly faster growth than estimated.

Nearly one out of every two people on the Internet visits YouTube and if YouTube were a country, it'd be the third largest in the world after China and India!

Wow and double Wow!! Do you think you should get involved?

Some people walk through the house making a little video on their smart phones and giving commentary. This can sometimes work but *can* look a little shaky with poor sound = amateurish.

We use www.animoto.com to create simple and short but really effective videos for advertising our properties. There is a free option and it's really easy to use once you get the hang of it. You can upload videos to Spareroom.com and post a link to that video on EasyRoomMate.com.

If you want something a little slicker and upmarket, ask someone on People Per Hour to professionally edit your photos and words to create a compelling video with your branding included etc.

With this option you can have images fading in and out with or without commentary. You can add words to the video to make sure the message is load and clear. You could also add one liner testimonials – this is always powerful.

It's better to get involved sooner than later - do not ignore this Tip :-)

#34 'Owning' Your Patch

One of the best ways to find those hidden deals in your area, is to spend time actually 'in' your goldmine area walking the streets and meeting people.

There is only so much you can do and see on Rightmove. If you don't like walking or don't have the time – get the bike out!

We found one brilliant deal by just talking to people and another that we spotted behind another property that we would otherwise have driven straight past. Have a conversation with the local shopkeeper, the postman, home owners in the area – do some detective work and even offer a cash incentive if they were to find you a deal.

We offer £500. The general idea is to know your 'patch' better than your local agent knows it! You also get some exercise!

#35 If it Moves, Systemise it!

It's all well and good to be told this but sometimes you don't quite know what to systemise and even how to do it! A simple way to think of it is 'What can I Delegate, Automate or Eliminate?' In our office we all have this little mantra on post-it notes, stuck to the side of our computer screens as a constant reminder.

Since applying this *radical* thought process to *EVERYTHING* we do, we have found that not only has life become easier, it's also become much more productive! Think 'DAE' and start to document everything you do. Then at the end of the day or week take a look over your notes to see how you can improve your systems. Also try talking to more experienced investors to see what they do.

S.Y.S.T.E.M.

Saves You Stress Time Energy and Money.

I (Francis) tried implementing it into my relationship with only limited success!! Doh!

Seriously, that last thing you want to do it to create another really busy and stressful job for yourself. Get into the habit of thinking DAE and make sure you have time to holiday after all that hard work!

We all love bullet pointed lists (don't we?) and with this in mind we have created a booklet full of lists of every process we carry out in our MLCS Rent 2 Rent business, from first viewing the property to signing the tenants in, all the daily management issues to handing a property back.

That booklet is called Rent 2 Rent Secrets.

This little booklet contains top secret and highly valuable information that took a long time to work out and compile. It is something that we rarely share outside of our MLCS community and is therefore only available to people who have completed our flagship training day. Join our community and its almost free!

Check it out here:

www.MultiLetCashflowSystem.com/Manual

#36 Email Signatures

Technically this is not really a Multi-let tip, but it is a good, free and consistent bit of marketing.

This will ensure that everyone you email will be reminded of your brand. So many people stick with their original Gmail, Yahoo or hotmail addresses, and this is such a wasted marketing opportunity. Each email you send could also be an advert of who you are or a link to your website, which will in turn drive more business your way. Why would you 'not' do it?

I (Francis) was asking someone why they didn't have a proper email signature and he seriously said he really liked saying 'Yahoo'! Okkkaaayyy!

My email address is francis@multiletcashflowsystem.com, it's the same for all the team, but of course with their first name. We think addresses that start with info@ or admin@ are too impersonal as people prefer the personal touch these days. Every time we send an email we advertise our websites and there is an image of some of our books. You may want to add a photo of your shiny face to yours (unless you have a good face for the radio?) or your website branding. Be consistant.

While you're at it remember to personalise your voicemail!

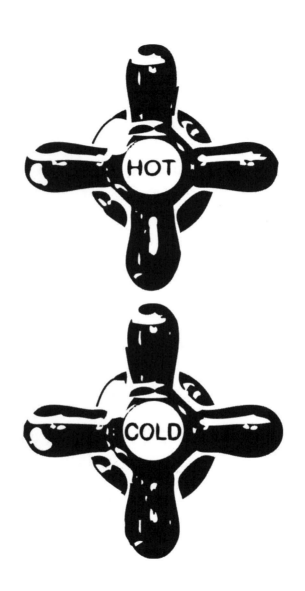

116

#37 Fire and Ice

Some people start sweating buckets when the temperature rises to 16 degrees, whilst others reach for their thermals and *onesies* (which are wrong on so many levels!) when it drops below 25 degrees! We try to maintain a steady 20 degrees in our properties and set the thermostats to switch on between 6 and 9am and then again between 4 and 10pm. We insulate all lofts (you can get grants), and tell tenants to be sensible and wear layers of clothing.

Hive Active Heating is designed to save energy and money, by setting up your heating and hot water system to make it as efficient as possible. If you have a combi boiler you can control your heating, and if you have a traditional boiler with a hot water tank you can control your heating and hot water.

The kit is professionally installed alongside your existing heating system by a British Gas engineer. You can control your heating and hot water on your smartphone or laptop (anytime anywhere), and there's no need to switch your energy supplier.

The Receiver is the Hive brain and is installed close to your boiler, the receiver lets your boiler and thermostat communicate with each other. The Hub box simply plugs into your broadband router so your thermostat can connect to the internet and be controlled remotely. Log on to the website and you can see the temperature inside your home for the last day, week, month or even year. If you want to make a change, just send your command in a text message to Hive.

You can use it to help spot when your heating may have been on when tenants weren't at home or if they're leaving the heating on overnight.

Add up to 5 additional users and they can control your heating & hot water using text control too. You can set and reset the 4 digit PIN with the app or on the website.

The installation is from £150 (if you have a gas account with them). If you have multiple houses you should get further installations for £99 each.

Check out the website www.HiveHome.com

Due to the forever changing landscape and the interpretation of new legislation, it is unclear at the time of going to print, as to whether or not you are still able to place a cap on monthly Multi-Let household bills. We have always capped our gas and electric bills combined at £200. A great website to help you stay up to date with property law is www.landlordlaw.co.uk.

#38 Tenant Demographics

Mixing household ages does not usually work – the mindset of a 25 year old is somewhat different from that of a 45 year old. That said, we have on occasion mixed ages successfully, but then on the other hand, when it goes wrong, it goes spectacularly wrong!

So these days we stick mostly to 'young' professionals in the 25 to 35 age range. When we have someone on the phone who sounds a little older we just mention that the average age of the house is 28 (?), *'Will that be a good fit for you?'* This way you don't have to ask their age out straight and upset anyone.

With more and more people choosing to live on their own, we are considering setting up a few properties for the 35+ age group. A friend of ours has a house full of divorced dads that he has christened *'The Dads for Justice House'!*

Top tip - Older tenants generally stay much longer as they see it as more of a permanent home. If you have any long term tenants who are happy and really care for their environment, you could let them choose the household decor/items themselves and reimburse them the money. This makes them feel it's their home and that they truly belong!

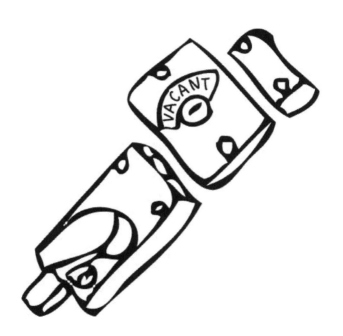

#39 Getting Engaged

This is a small but crucial tip and your tenants will love you for fitting these little bathroom locks!

You can't always tell if the smallest room in the house is being used until you try the door handle, and some sensitive people find this a little uncomfortable.

For £6 your tenants will be able to tell at a glance if the bathroom is free or not. Available from most hardware stores including B&Q or online at www.ironmongerydirect.co.uk

#40 Bite The Rent-Pro Bullet

If you are really frugal (tight) when it comes to recurring payments leaving your bank account you might want to stick to excel spreadsheets as they are free. Nothing wrong with that is they are working well for you. But as you grow you may decide to bite the bullet and switch to Rent Pro management software – it's a great system and it's the only one we could find with specific programmes for using with Rent 2 Rent, as it calculates using a 'rent', and not a per-centage.

Rent-Pro is cloud based with bank-level security (we think this is a good thing!) and normally cost £65 pcm, but we have negotiated a deal whereby you can get it for £50 pcm – just quote this code Promo Code – 50MLCS50.

It is great for payments, statements, correspondence, customised reports, letters and logo's, plus a host of other features. When the time comes you will regret that you didn't switch over sooner! Doh!!

Newsflash -as we are going to print we have just discovered another system that is looking great and is totally free. We are currently testing this – subscribe to our email newsletter for updates.

#41 What Are They Hiding?

Pesky and time consuming as it may be, you must reference your tenants in some way, shape or form.

We do our referencing in-house as its faster and cheaper. We call the applicants employers and previous landlord, ask to see ID and their NI card and ask our set questions. One of which is *'Can I see 3 months bank statements please'*, as this will tell you soooo much.

1. That they have a job and where
2. They can afford the rent
3. Are good with their money and
4. Have paid the last 3 months' rent.

If they were ever going to not pay the rent it will be at the end of their last tenancy.

A quick and easy way to check up on your tenants, that a lot of guys forget about, is to simply Google the applicant and check them out on Facebook! Bear in mind that they can do the same checks on you – so better clean up that FB profile!

If you haven't got a copy already, check out 'The 14 Killer Questions to ask a tenant' from the Endless Tenants Mini-Manual. available here;

www.multiletcashflowsystem.com/manual

If you do want to go down the full reference route, then a company that we have found to be excellent is Advanced Rent.

www.AdvancedRent.co.uk offer excellent and really fast referencing amongst many other services. They have been creating products specifically aimed at the Rent 2 Rent market as they see massive growth in this area over the coming years. If you contact them via the MLCS website you will gain a further discount.

Another company – www.RentChecks.com – claim to be the only UK company with direct links to the Government immigration department database. This has become a serious matter, as landlords we are now liable if we rent our rooms to illegal immigrants! We think it would be better if the border police just did their job!

#42 Hey! It's Maintenance Month

We do regular interim inspections throughout the year – every 3 months. We take a clipboard and make a note of every little job that needs doing. Any urgent jobs we do immediately, other jobs we put on the 'Maintenance Month' list. We found that by grouping tasks together we saved a *LOT* of time.

When maintenance month comes around, we have a list of jobs for each house, all the materials bought and ready to go and most importantly we are focused on the jobs. If we need to meet any tradesmen, that too has been arranged. We found that jumping from little repair job to little repair job was eating up way too much time – this way is much more efficient.

We never get customer complaints as we spot potential problems before they arise and this is a great way to do business.

Remember it's all about, *minimum input for maximum output!*

#43 Coca-Cola
Vs
Alka-Seltzer

A quick one.

Coca-Cola and Alka-Seltzer are often cited as the best toilet cleaners on the market!

Try them and see for yourself! Tie the ball-cock up so that the toilet won't refill when you flush it, then fill it up with Cola etc. Leave them overnight for maximum results.

This does beg the question . . . 'what on earth are they doing to your stomach'!!??

#44 Listen to Your Gut!

'Cause your gut is usually right!

An empty room is better than being stuck with a bad non-paying tenant and a pending eviction case! No one likes that kind of stress. If you have a bad feeling about someone, you're probably right. If you are not sure, do a full reference including a credit check and always get a guarantor for any tenants that don't quite fit your strict criteria.

As per tip 41, if you use www.AdvancedRent.co.uk, they will inform you of any tenant arrears or any damage the tenant may have caused – all uploaded to their system by their previous landlords.

If you have an empty room that's proving difficult to shift, don't be tempted to accept a 'dodgy character' just to save money. If you do have a small void, use this opportunity to do all the improvements and make the property more presentable for achieving the best rent you were after in the first place. How can you make your rooms irresistible?

#45 Why You *MUST* Dress Your Rooms

Fact; Dressed rooms always go first!

As long as the house is well presented, clean/tidy and the price is right, you can let any room. When a room is empty it can look forlorn and somewhat unloved, and may lead to multiple viewings and lots of wasted time.

We always dress rooms ready for showing with a nice duvet and matching pillow set, hang a few pictures, possibly a rug and some plastic flowers if we're feeling frivolous!

We sometimes put a lamp on the bedside table and if needed plug in an air-freshener to create a nice mood in the room. Make sure the room is sparkling clean including the windows. This 'room kit' fits neatly into one of those big plastic bags you get from Ikea. We now have several 'room dressing kits'!

We don't leave items in the bedrooms – that would get very expensive (unless the tenant offers to buy it) but we do dress the communal area of the property and that kit stays.

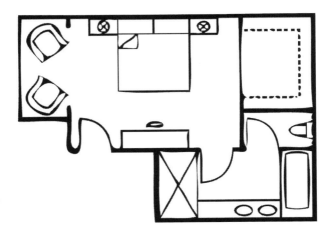

#46 How to Rent That Small Room

We had one property with a small room that was always difficult to fill, so we put ourselves in the tenant's position . . . what would they find irresistible?

We eBay'ed a 24" TV with free-view for £25, upgraded to some heavier designer curtains and furniture, got a cool(small) rug, a big canvas of a sunny beach (that looked like an extra window and gave the room depth) and asked our handyman to build in a small desk – it was just big enough to fit a laptop and a coffee cup.

Now it's a cool looking room and no longer sticks!

It is common belief that the smallest rentable room is 6.5Sq M but this is actually only a guideline (for most councils). If there is adequate space in the rest of the house then smaller rooms are permitted. Check with your local council officer (who may be unsure).

We gifted the TV to the new tenant so that we wouldn't be responsible for the TV license. We supply one TV license per household.

#47 1737 Was a Very Good Year

Once or twice we have had tenants give notice, and have the new occupant all ready to move in that very same day. Then the existing tenant says he has a problem and will be staying for another week! Agghh!

This once meant we had to pay for a French gentleman to move into a B&B for the week at great expense to us and the gentleman was not too pleased either!

If we wanted to evict the existing tenant we would have had to go through a laborious court procedure, which would have taken longer than a week anyway!

Frustrating.

Then we stumbled upon a thoroughly lovely and obscure piece of legislation called the Distress for Rent Act 1737.

The fantastic old law came into force in the reign of King George II, and allows a landlord to charge a naughty tenant double the rent on a daily basis for each and every day they remain in the property after you have ended their tenancy.

At last, a law that favours the poor old landlord! If only we had known about it when we needed it!

We think that this ancient law has been 'overlooked' and could be repealed at any moment, so keep it to yourself until you need it) ;-)

Would you actually use it?

Debatable, but it's a lovely bit of legislation that may persuade the departing tenant to head for a mates couch.

Just Google 'Distress for Rent Act 1737'.

#48 Learn to Outsource ASAP

This Top Tip is HUGE!

You know the old saying that *no man is an island*.

If there was ever any industry where this applies, it would be the property industry.

You may manage to get that first property up and running completely singlehandedly, doing all the sourcing, raising finance, negotiation, refurbishment, dressing the rooms, conducting viewings, taking care of all the paperwork – the list goes on and on. But if you want your business to grow, at some point or another you will need help.

So why not bring in part time team members from day one? We now employ 10 part-time team members from all corners of the planet, on an ad-hoc basis as and when we need them. There are many on-line websites such as Fiverr.com, PeoplePerHour.com and AllDayPA.com.

You will also have all your favourite Agents and tradesmen on speed dial and if you have your copy of *Employing Your Property Manager*, you will already know how to outsource many of the day to day jobs.

Remember to think;

'Delegate, Outsource, Automate'

. . . and last of all, 'Do'.

This way you won't create another all-consuming job for yourself.

Look at the big picture, after all what are you *really* doing this for, and anyway it's more fun being part of a team. You will have someone to bounce ideas around with and best of all, someone to celebrate your many successes with.

#49 Filling Rooms Via Text

Filling your rooms can end up being a huge hassle if you haven't got your systems in place. One thing we started to do a long time ago that has increased the speed and ease in which we fill rooms, is keeping a database of potential tenants.

We now keep the name and phone number of everyone who contacts us who interested in a room. This means that when we take on a new house or have a room become available we are able to send mass texts to everyone who is interested.

In the past this has enabled us to fill a 5 bed house within 3 days of getting the keys! We have heard of some guys 'harvesting' the phone numbers of potentials tenants by placing a fake ad of a brilliant looking room/house with a much lower than usual rent. They then save all the contact details and when they DO have a vacancy they offer £25 to £50 as a finder's fee. This way they are constantly building their data base.

Take a look at www.mightytext.net

You should have a facility for people to unsubscribe from your list.

WHATEVER IS GOOD
FOR YOUR SOUL. .DO THAT.

#50 Wooo Hooo - Free Electric

Free?! It's never really free- there's always a catch . . . isn't there?

If you are like us, you've probably seen Solar Panels on roofs all over the UK, right? You may have also considered getting some on your own, or your rental properties?

You may also know about the grants available to homeowners? But like us you might have stopped short of installing them, as you heard it takes many years to recoup your initial cost!

Well, we came across a company that *claimed* to do your installation absolutely, completely, 100% free! This includes supplying all equipment and labour, and could also include free loft and cavity installation if needed.

The cost of the installation is actually £10k, but if you stay in the property or keep the property for 5 years you may wipe this cost. Alternatively, persuade 5 of your smartest friends to also have the panels installed and the original installation is totally free.

We have recently installed a system on one of our properties and it is already paying for itself. We also took advantage the free loft and cavity installation.

So we think it is worth your time and of course it is also good for your soul!

Do your due diligence and fish around to find a reliable, insurance backed company.

Nowadays we get Utility Warehouse bills that are in credit, which means that the company pays US money to use THEIR electric.

We always thought this was an urban myth!

We like this a lot as it means more holidays!

#51 Sex Up Your Inventories

We are currently working on a 100% hands-off system that will allow tenants to create their own inventories without us even being present. Why? We find that quite a few tenants want to move into a property outside of our normal business hours, and whilst we are keen to help and are hungry for 100% full rooms, it does have an impact on our social lives.

So picture this. New tenant arrives on a Sunday evening. Collects keys from Key Safe by punching in the numbers we had texted them earlier. They open our inventory app on their phone and electronically tick the boxes. If they do not agree with the condition of, say the carpet, they take a photo, log it and carry on with the inventory.

This system is so cool, it's icy and is currently work in progress. Watch this space.

Until then we will carry on doing in-house 'normal' inventories – which for us is a one page, detailing the communal areas and a further page detailing the condition of the bedroom. Some people prefer to use an outside company as the validity of in-house inventories 'could' be challenged in court.

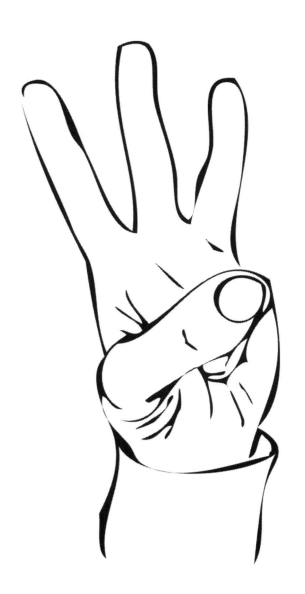

#52 Hard Wired
For Success

Meaning 1;

By law you must do an annual safety check of ALL portable appliances in your properties and get a portable appliance test (PAT) certificate for each house. If you have a lot of appliances and a lot of properties this can soon mount up.

To reduce these reoccurring costs, some landlord's hard-wire portable appliances straight into the main with a fused spur. This is perfectly safe and legal and circumnavigates PAT's (in some areas, check with your council)

Meaning 2;

Remember our promise to you at the front of this little book of 52 Tips? We said it would help you become 3 x's more efficient and 3 x's more successful a landlord than you were before you read it! We said they will help you save money and help you make money! We sincerely hope this has worked out well for you.

In your business you should constantly strive for *minimum input for maximum output,* and the implementation of some or all of these Top Tips will certainly helped you create a successful and smooth running property portfolio.

The final word

It's OK to focus on yields and ROI's, but we must always remember that property is a people business and we must respect our customers (tenants) needs, respond to complaints fast and provide a safe, warm and clean environment.

Be an industry leader like Steve Jobs, be proud of what you do and it will undoubtedly hard-wire you for success!

Do this and the money will naturally follow.

If you have any brilliant Top Multi-Let Tips you think would be of benefit to UK landlords, please send them over to us to include in edition 2.

You can also send your property friends a link to www.52MultiLetTips.com, they will thank you for it!

Happy investing!

About the Authors

52 Multi-let Tips was put together by Francis and Emily Dolley with the assistance of their property manager Will Matthews.

Francis, who had been working in the construction industry and dabbling in property investing for a number of years, was very pleased when his daughter Emily decided she wanted to work with him in their family business.

They needed to drastically increase their cash-flow really quickly and so entered the fast-paced and lucrative world of Rent 2 Rent investing.

Unlike traditional investing you do not need a huge mortgage or a hefty deposit. Properties can sometimes be set up and cash-flowing in a matter of days.

Francis and Emily have now perfected their systems so that they can sometimes control the properties for nearly zero input and get them set up and tenanted a matter of days after the viewing. This means the business is 100% pure profit almost from day one!

But of course the last thing they wanted was to create another busy job for themselves, so they started building a team. An integral member of the team is Will, who has created a phenomenal record of no voids from day one of his employment and continues to be an asset in every area of the business as it grows from strength to strength.

Francis and Emily now run training days where you can find out more about the Multi-Let Cashflow System and how *YOU* can *Turbo-Charge your Cashflow with Multi-Lets*.

As well as training many hundreds of people the correct way to invest in Rent 2 Rent, Francis and Emily have also created a brilliant community of like minded souls all on the same path.

This is a highly supportive group who meet regularly and often celebrate their successes.

Maybe you would like to join us.

www.MultiLetCashflowSystem.com

More Stuff!

You can also check out:

www.MayhemMurderandMultiLets.com

www.FrancisDolley.com

www.MLCSEDGE.com

Oh, we have one more Top Tip . . .

Make sure you have some fun along the way!

Happy investing!!

Francis & Emily